ANSWERED PRAYERS

Jeremiah 33:3 Call unto me, and I will answer thee, and shew thee great and mighty things, which thou knowest not.

LEO R. LAVINKA

Copyright © 2019 by Leo R. LaVinka
All Rights Reserved
Printed in the United States of America
August, 2019

REL067030: Religion: Christian Theology – Apologetics.

ISBN 978-1-7339247-5-7

All Scripture quotes are from the King James Bible.

No part of this work may be reproduced without the expressed consent of the publisher, except for brief quotes, whether by electronic, photocopying, recording, or information storage and retrieval systems.

Address All Inquiries To:
THE OLD PATHS PUBLICATIONS, Inc.
142 Gold Flume Way
Cleveland, Georgia, U.S.A. 30528

Web: www.theoldpathspublications.com
E-mail: TOP@theoldpathspublications.com

1.0

DEDICATION

I dedicate this book to Ray Owens who left this earth for heaven on January 29, 1997. He was my friend and prayer partner for over twenty-five years. He was a faithful man of God who always served his church and God to the very best of his ability. He set a very high standard in his testimony as a husband, father, and faithful servant. It was my blessing that God allowed me to know and serve with this faithful servant of God.

FOREWORD

My book, *"Are You Ready,"* was written for the purpose of passing on to my descendants a testimony of some Biblical essentials necessary for salvation and growing in faith for born again Christians. It contains six topics which I believe would help as the clear preaching of God's Word, at least in our nation, grows colder and colder. Hopefully, it will motivate all readers to search all the scripture, study it, hide it in their heart, meditate on it, obey it, and live by it.

> *Psalm 78:5-7 For he established a testimony in Jacob, and appointed a law in Israel, which he commanded our fathers, that they should make them known to their children: 6 That the generation to come might know them, even the children which should be born; who should arise and declare them to their children: 7 That they might set their hope in God, and not forget the works of God, but keep his commandments:*

> *Psalm 9:17 The wicked shall be turned into hell, and all the nations that forget God.*

On further reflection I discovered one very important topic was left out. That is God's desire to hear our petitions (prayers) and answer them in accordance with His perfect will. He is our Father; we are His sons. I am convinced we do not receive many of the blessings He offers because we don't ask or really believe He will answer. We know He can, we just don't believe He will. When we do get answers we won't give God the credit and glory that he richly deserves. We shrug it off as coincidence.

> *Psalm 107:8 Oh that men would praise the LORD for his goodness, and for his wonderful works to the children of men!*

> *John 1:12 But as many as received him, to them gave he power to become the sons of God, even to them that believe on his name.*

This book, *"Answered Prayers,"* reflects a few of the numerous prayers I personally know God has answered. My desire is that our Holy God will receive all the glory for the wonderful care and personal attention He bestows on all of us as His family, the Church of God. To God be the glory!

Jeremiah 33:3 Call unto me, and I will answer thee, and shew thee great and mighty things, which thou knowest not.

TABLE OF CONTENTS

DEDICATION 3
FOREWORD 5
TABLE OF CONTENTS 9
INTRODUCTION 11
    TO GOD BE THE GLORY 13
    GOD ANSWERS PRAYERS..................................... 14
    WAREHOUSE OF BLESSINGS 16
    SEEK AND YOU WILL FIND 17
    GROWING IN FAITH 18
    PERSONAL CONVICTION 19
    TRACT MINISTRY 21
    LOST FOR GOD 23
    LED BY GOD... 24
    KEEP ON KEEPING ON 25
    ONE MORE DOOR.. 26
    TEACH YOUR CHILDREN 27
    JESUS LOVES CHILDREN..................................... 28
    OUR SATURDAY NIGHT PRAYER MEETING.......... 30
    RAY OWENS FAITHFULNESS............................... 31
    PRAYERS ANSWERED 32
    THE HOLY SPIRIT GUIDES.................................... 33
    BREEDLOVE'S CHRISTMAS GIFT 35
    CURTIS HUTSON - GOAL SETTER 36
    ENCOURAGE OTHERS... 37
    HUTSON/HATCH REVIVAL 38
    KEEPING PLEDGE 39
    BROKEN PLEDGE 40
    FORREST HILL BAPTIST CHURCH PARKING LOT. 41
    CHASTENING OF GOD.. 43
    CHRISTIAN SCHOOL.. 44
    MARTA'S ROUTE CHANGED BY PRAYER 47
    MARTA VS. CHURCH 48
    PROPERTY FOUND 49
    BIG DREAMS.. 52
    SEWAGE LIFT STATION PROBLEM 54
    SATAN'S INTERFERENCE 55
    PROPERTY DEVELOPMENT................................. 57
    PRAYERS ANSWERED 58

DREAM WITH THE PREACHER 60
SHATTERED DREAMS 61
CORINTH BAPTIST CHURCH 62
SAVED BY GOING SOUL WINNING..................... 62
GOD'S MIRACLES.. 64
MARVIN SAVED 65
GOD CALLS OUR PREACHER................................ 66
PRAYER CHAIN FOR JANE.................................... 67
ELSIE CURED 68
FORBID THEM NOT 69
PRAY FOR KATHRYN 70
MIRACLE FROM BRAZIL 73
FAITH BAPTIST CHURCH 75
SITTING DUCK 76
VISION RESTORED 77
NO CANCER 78
HOPE RESTORED 79
DELAYED PRAYER.. 81
MOUNTAIN MOVED.. 83
AN ANSWER TO PRAYER BY AN AMAZING GOD. . 84
OUR CREATOR HAS NO LIMITS 87
DOERS OF THE WORD.. 88
FAITH... 91
SCRIPTURE REFERENCES FOR THE POEM, "FAITH" By LEO LAVINKA 93
SCRIPTURE REFERENCES IN THE BOOK................. 96
INDEX 98
ABOUT THE AUTHOR... 112

INTRODUCTION

How many prayers have you received an answer from God and did not give him credit? One or two, maybe hundreds, or even thousands. Why do many people pray morning and night bringing their worship, praise, and petitions to God, and really don't think He is listening? When we do see specific answers we shrug it off thinking it's a coincidence. We are grateful for the answer, but won't give God credit for his intervention. Does this sound familiar? I am personally convicted of my own short comings in not giving God his due credit and praise in answering my prayers. Job had a desire that his words were written, printed in a book, and graven with an iron pen and lead in the rock forever. He said in Job 19:25, 26 *"For I know that my redeemer liveth, and that he shall stand at the latter day upon the earth: and though my skin worms destroy this body, yet in my flesh shall I see God."* Job got his prayers answered. His words are recorded in the Bible (KJV) and are forever settled in heaven, and he has now seen God. Job's prayers should be our own prayer with respect to answered prayers as well as all our other thousands of blessings.

> *Job 19:23-24 Oh that my words were now written! oh that they were printed in a book! 24 That they were graven with an iron pen and lead in the rock for ever!*

This book is my feeble attempt to bring to the attention of those who read it that our God is a loving God who cares for us and has even numbered the hairs on our head. His attributes are infinitely larger than our ability to comprehend or understand. This book only addresses "Answered Prayers," and I write it knowing full well that there is no way I can even scratch the surface of recording how great God is in hearing and answering our prayers. May we give God all praise and glory. He alone is awesome and deserves all our gratitude, praise, and worship. To God be the glory!

> *John 21:25 And there are also many other things which Jesus did, the which, if they should be written every one, I suppose that even the world itself could not contain the books that should be written. Amen.*

I also want to acknowledge the help of my faithful wife, and Dr. and Mrs. H. D.

Williams for their assistance in producing this book. To God be the glory!

TO GOD BE THE GLORY

The Bible (KJV) teaches us to pray without ceasing. Jesus said ask (pray) in faith nothing wavering. Pastor Terry Poole said, "Most of us believe God can answer prayer, we just don't believe He will." When we do pray and God answers do we really give God his due credit, praise, and glory? If God's heart could be broken, this should do it. Jesus said we have not because we ask not. God is our Father. We are His children. Would a father give his child a stone if he asked for bread or a serpent if he asked for a fish? Would you? Christrians who are <u>right</u> with God and pray <u>do</u> get answers. How many Christians looking back would say as Job did *"Oh that my words were now written _ _ printed in a book! _ _graven in the rock for ever!."* I believe most of us could apply Job's prayer with our own desire concerning answered prayers; "Oh that they were remembered and recorded for all to see."; to give God all the praise and glory that he so richly deserves; to show that our redeemer lives and he is a loving Father who cares for us.

Matthew 7:7-10 Ask, and it shall be given you; seek, and ye shall find; knock, and it shall be opened unto you: 8 For every one that asketh receiveth; and he that seeketh findeth; and to him that knocketh it shall be opened. 9 Or what man is there of you, whom if his son ask bread, will he give him a stone? 10 Or if he ask a fish, will he give him a serpent?

James 1:6-7 But let him ask in faith, nothing wavering. For he that wavereth is like a wave of the sea driven with the wind and tossed. 7 For let not that man think that he shall receive any thing of the Lord.

Matthew 21:22 And all things, whatsoever ye shall ask in prayer, believing, ye shall receive.

James 4:3 Ye ask, and receive not, because ye ask amiss, that ye may consume it upon your lusts.

GOD ANSWERS PRAYERS

There are many books available on prayer. John R. Rice wrote a book titled *"Prayer, Asking and Receiving."* He said the answer to prayer is receiving. Many books discuss hindrances to prayer, how to pray, what to pray for, etc. If you want your prayers answered, keep God's commandments, live to please God, and receive the joy of the Lord. This book is written to reveal God's answering prayers in my own personal life, and the lives of friends. It only gives a small sample of what I remember and certainly doesn't reflect the many that I have forgotten, but every now and then they pop into my mind. I want my family, their descendants, and all who read this book to know our one true God is a loving Father who has a bag of blessings available to all who ask. I am not a Bible scholar, nor do I claim to be a prayer warrior. I am only a child of God bought and paid for by the precious blood of Jesus Christ.

> *1John 3:22 And whatsoever we ask, we receive of him, because we keep his commandments, and do those things that are pleasing in his sight.*
>
> *John 16:24 Hitherto have ye asked nothing in my name: ask, and ye shall receive, that your joy may be full.*

> *Luke 11:10 For every one that asketh receiveth; and he that seeketh findeth; and to him that knocketh it shall be opened.*
>
> *Psalm 66:18 If I regard iniquity in my heart, the Lord will not hear me.*

WAREHOUSE OF BLESSINGS

This book has absolutely nothing to do with me. It is meant to give God all the praise and glory which He richly deserves. Not to do so could only bring the wrath of God on all of us; but thanks be to God who loves us. He is God! I'm a nobody except for the redeeming blood of my Lord and Savior, Jesus Christ. My prayer is that all who read this will only see God and his <u>love</u> for all his children. I once heard a preacher describe our lack of prayer by saying when we get to heaven we may see a large warehouse full of blessings which God had for each of us if we had only asked. To God be the glory for answering our prayers.

> *Acts 12:23 And immediately the angel of the Lord smote him, because he gave not God the*

glory: and he was eaten of worms, and gave up the ghost.

Romans 11:36 For of him, and through him, and to him, are all things: to whom be glory for ever. Amen.

1 John 4:8 He that loveth not knoweth not God; for God is love.

Ephesians 2:4 But God, who is rich in mercy, for his great love wherewith he loved us,

SEEK AND YOU WILL FIND

I think my first sincere prayer may have been standing over my friend's grave realizing that life was short, and that I could have been the one in the grave instead of my friend. I had a heart felt concern for life after death. I asked God to reveal his truth. I discussed this with my wife and we started seeking God's truth. We started going to a Methodist Church, but it didn't help. Finally, my job transferred from Jacksonville, Florida to Atlanta, Georgia where a co-worker, Bob Carpenter, continuously bombarded me with scripture and his personal testimony. He was different. He always demonstrated his love, commitment, peace of mind, and dedication to serving God. I wanted what he had. He invited me to Forrest Hills Baptist Church where Curtis Hutson was pastor. After much preaching and my friend's continuous concern, my wife and I on August 24, 1969, prayed for forgiveness and asked Jesus Christ to save us. He did! God answers prayer!

> *Luke 11:9 And I say unto you, Ask, and it shall be given you; seek, and ye shall find; knock, and it shall be opened unto you.*
>
> *John 3:16 For God so loved the world, that he gave his only begotten Son, that whosoever believeth in him should not perish, but have everlasting life.*
>
> *Romans 10:13 For whosoever shall call upon the name of the Lord shall be saved.*

GROWING IN FAITH

The instant I got saved I wanted to grow in the Lord and tell others, especially my family, what God did for me. I began to grow under the great ministry of Pastor

Curtis Hutson and many other great visiting preachers.

> *Romans 10:17 So then faith cometh by hearing, and hearing by the word of God.*
>
> *2 Corinthians 5:17 Therefore if any man be in Christ, he is a new creature: old things are passed away; behold, all things are become new.*
>
> *2 Timothy 3:16-17 All scripture is given by inspiration of God, and is profitable for doctrine, for reproof, for correction, for instruction in righteousness: That the man of God may be perfect, throughly furnished unto all good works.*

PERSONAL CONVICTION

Forrest Hills Baptist Church had many great people who lived their testimony. Visitation and tract distribution were emphasized. I became convicted of my lack of service. I thought when I know my Bible like others, and when I was not scared of questions, or praying in public I too would give out tracts and go visiting. It finally dawned on me I would <u>never</u> go. I gave up and prayed to God for help. He said go and depend completely on Him to do the work. This partnership worked. Just pray and go. I still go visiting and pass out tracts. I can't save anyone but my God can and does. God answers prayers!

> *Romans 1:16 For I am not ashamed of the gospel of Christ: for it is the power of God unto salvation to every one that believeth; to the Jew first, and also to the Greek.*
>
> *Matthew 28:18-20 And Jesus came and spake unto them, saying, All power is given unto me in heaven and in earth. Go ye therefore, and teach all nations, baptizing them in the name of the Father, and of the Son, and of the Holy Ghost: Teaching them to observe all things whatsoever I have commanded you: and, lo, I am with you alway, even unto the end of the world. Amen.*
>
> *Luke 19:10 For the Son of man is come to seek and to save that which was lost.*

TRACT MINISTRY

Passing out tracts at the Atlanta Airport in those days was easy. You were allowed to go anywhere short of actually boarding an airplane. If you wore a dark suit people must have thought you were an employee of the airport. We would take a large box of tracts, stand at the top of an escalator, and pass them out as fast as we could reach into the box for another handful. The tract was excellent. It was a little book titled "How to get around in the Atlanta Airport." It contained a map, directions, puzzles, and the Plan of Salvation. I feel sure that anyone receiving this information from one whom they thought was an employee would read every page. It was that well prepared. Thousands of these tracts were passed out by this process. Tracts coupled with prayer do have an impact on all who read them. To God be the glory. God answers prayer.

James 4:17 Therefore to him that knoweth to do good, and doeth it not, to him it is sin.

We also passed out tracts in all the Atlanta area. One was titled "How to get to Heaven from Atlanta, Georgia." If you have traveled much on airlines you would be aware of Atlanta being a major hub for air travel and would appreciate this tract.

Passing out tracts at the Olympics in Atlanta in 1996 was easier yet. I worked in downtown Atlanta, and at noon would pass out two special tracts. They each had a cover depicting the Olympics. One was the "Gospel of John." The other tract was "How to be Saved." I had two shoulder bags containing these tracts. By having my hands free I could give both tracts out at the same time to each person. People would actually start falling in line to receive these tracts. It was very difficult to keep up with the line. These tracts were carried around the world from visitors to the Olympics. Our church prayed for God to receive glory at the Olympics. To God be the glory. God answers prayer.

> *Isaiah 55:11 So shall my word be that goeth forth out of my mouth: it shall not return unto me void, but it shall accomplish that which I please, and it shall prosper in the thing whereto I sent it.*

LOST FOR GOD

As I have said passing out tracts was emphasized by Pastor Hutson. Metro Atlanta and its suburbs were saturated with tracts. One Wednesday evening service I went to church alone. My wife was home with sick children. Pastor Hutson preached and asked everyone to take seven tracts and pass them out before we went home. To be honest I did not feel up to it. After all I had to get up early to go to work. (Does this sound familiar?) My devious mind began to think how I could pass out seven tracts with the least amount of time and effort. I had driven the same route to my home many times. Just before getting on the Interstate highway was an apartment complex. I thought that's the place. I can (without knocking) place seven tracts on seven doors and be gone in minutes. God had other plans. I unknowingly made a wrong turn and before I realized it I was in a rundown neighborhood with many people sitting on their porch, some walking on the sidewalks, and a few groups just talking under the street lights. A car close behind me was all I needed to convince me to flee this neighborhood. Since I was thoroughly familiar with all the surrounding area I knew

I would come to a familiar location. I drove over a railroad track that totally confused me because I was very familiar with <u>every</u> crossing, but could <u>not</u> identify this one. I drove on and kept turning in the direction that I thought would free me from my maze. When I discovered my location I was at the same location where I first made the wrong turn. I was convicted! I prayed for help, drove back into the neighborhood, got out of my car, and started passing out tracts and witnessing to people. Seven people, by their testimony, trusted Christ and were saved. God answers prayer!

> *Luke 14:23 And the lord said unto the servant, Go out into the highways and hedges, and compel them to come in, that my house may be filled.*

LED BY GOD

On two separate occasions my partner and I attempted to visit the address given by a visitor to our church. We had the address but when we arrived we found an apartment complex with many apartments in numerous buildings. We did not have the apartment number. We prayed for God to lead us to the right apartment. We chose a building and an apartment. In both cases it was the right apartment. God answers prayer!

> *Psalm 121:1-2 I will lift up mine eyes unto the hills, from whence cometh my help. My help cometh from the LORD, which made heaven and earth.*

KEEP ON KEEPING ON

On another occasion my partner and I visited thirty apartments (by count) in an apartment complex. We had absolutely no results and we could not understand why. It was 9:00 p.m. which was getting late for door knocking. We prayed and asked God to help us if we visited one more apartment. We did. We were invited in and were able to lead a man and wife to trust in Jesus Christ. God answers prayer!

> *Ephesians 5:20 Giving thanks always for all things unto God and the Father in the name of our Lord Jesus Christ.*

ONE MORE DOOR

One night a retired preacher and my friend, (Pastor John Reynold's dad), and I visited in an apartment complex until 9:00 p.m. Again absolutely no results. We concluded we were in the wrong place. We prayed and asked God's leadership to another location. We prayed that God would lead us to the right house if we made <u>one</u> more visit. I got lost in very familiar territory, but we thought God was leading. I turned down a street and we chose a house at random. We knocked on the door and a lady opened the door. We told her we were visiting from Forrest Hills Baptist Church. She immediately started crying. When she got control she told us she had been praying <u>that day</u> that someone would come <u>that night from "Forrest Hills Baptist Church"</u> to visit her. She only needed council and special prayer. God answers prayer (hers and ours)!

> *Hebrews 11:6 But without faith it is impossible to please him: for he that cometh to God must believe that he is, and that he is a rewarder of them that diligently seek him.*

TEACH YOUR CHILDREN

My wife and I have four children. We prayed many times that all of them would understand and trust Christ before their fifth birthday. Keep in mind we attended a great church (Forrest Hills Baptist Church) where salvation was clearly taught and we personally spent much time declaring the gospel to them. God answered our prayers, but our daughter Jane started crying during a church invitation and told me she wanted to be saved. I thought how could she be ready since she was not yet five years old. Like a fool I tried to convince her she was not ready, but her crying grew desperate. I suddenly realized that I could not decide the time or place for her. It must be conviction, repentance, understanding, and a call from the Holy Spirit. I took her forward, dealt with her, and <u>she trusted Christ</u>. Thank God for His Holy Word. A worst case scenario would be that she didn't get saved, but the seed would have been sown and she would not forget it. God answers prayer.

Proverbs 22:6 Train up a child in the way he should go: and when he is old, he will not depart from it.

Hebrews 7:25 Wherefore he is able also to save them to the uttermost that come unto God by him, seeing he ever liveth to make intercession for them.

Mark 10:14 But when Jesus saw it, he was much displeased, and said unto them, Suffer the little children to come unto me, and forbid them not: for of such is the kingdom of God.

JESUS LOVES CHILDREN

I know many would say a young child is too young to know what they are doing. I say keep sowing and tending the precious seed and it will root and sprout sooner than you think. I believe most of our problem is that we've been brainwashed into believing children are too young to understand to the extent we grossly neglect their early training. God help us! I'm currently singing "Jesus Loves Me" to our great grandchildren, ages 6, 4, 2, 1 and 5 weeks. The three oldest will sometimes sing or try to sing with me. The one-year-old will sometimes perk up and even sometimes stop crying when I try to sing. I tell them about Jesus every chance I get, even the youngest. I believe the older we get the harder it becomes to bow our knees to anyone. ("It's me that works and puts bread on the table.") Little children have total and complete trust in their parents for love, food, companionship, etc. They have faith and trust. I believe it's easier for them to understand faith and trust than it is for an older person. I believe the age of accountability (understanding sin and the penalty of sin) is the position one must be in to begin to understand and answer the call of the Holy Spirit. We need to teach young people so they will have a good foundation when that age occurs. I don't know how many times I have heard people say about the lost "I don't want to turn them off." When one is lost they are <u>already turned off</u>. One can only turn them <u>on</u>. We must use discernment.

> *Deuteronomy 6:6-7 And these words, which I command thee this day, shall be in thine heart: And thou shalt teach them diligently unto thy children, and shalt talk of them when thou sittest in thine house, and when thou walkest by the way, and when thou liest down, and when thou risest up.*

Isaiah 55:11 So shall my word be that goeth forth out of my mouth: it shall not return unto me void, but it shall accomplish that which I please, and it shall prosper in the thing whereto I sent it.

OUR SATURDAY NIGHT PRAYER MEETING

Pastor Curtis Hutson started a 24/7 prayer chain at our church. Church members signed a list to assure all hours were covered. It worked for several months but gradually there were only two members left, Ray Owens and myself. He and I finally joined together to pray at 9:00 p.m. every Saturday night. If one of us were absent due to work or sickness, the other one would be there. I can't recall any Saturday night that wasn't covered. This lasted until Ray's death twenty-five years later. I continued praying at our location until I joined another church a few years later.

1 Thessalonians 5:17 Pray without ceasing.

RAY OWENS FAITHFULNESS

Ray Owens was one of the most faithful men I have ever known. He was always very humble, meek, and kind. He was a faithful church worker at Forrest Hills Baptist Church who never complained. He served as treasurer, and performed many other tasks in our church. His wife told me they had never had an argument. I believe it. He was a man of habit, always the same. For example, he always ate a banana sandwich for lunch, never changing. He was very methodical and accurate in all his actions. A couple of habits he had did drive me crazy. Many times we would visit people or neighborhoods miles from our church in Atlanta, Georgia, and its suburbs. When we finished the visits if he was driving he would park under a street light and pull out a map to see the exact shortest way to return to the church. I would say, "Ray just take this route and it will lead us to the church." He would reply, "There may be a shorter way." When we would go on benevolence visits our budget was $20.00, enough in those days. This was before unit prices were displayed. He would figure the unit price for every item of every brand in his head to assure the best buy. Can you imagine how long it would take just to decide on a can of beans? I would tell Ray we will be here all night, and I would toss a few cans in the basket and move on. The only problem was when we got to the checkout counter I always had to pay an extra $20.00 or so. Ray was my friend and truly a great Christian. I miss him and still think of him.

> *Luke 14:11 For whosoever exalteth himself shall be abased; and he that humbleth himself shall be exalted.*

> *Proverbs 18:24 A man that hath friends must shew himself friendly: and there is a friend that sticketh closer than a brother.*

PRAYERS ANSWERED

Getting back to Ray and our prayer meetings. We saw many, many prayers answered. I can in no way remember even a fraction of them. We always prayed for things which we did not see an answer, but I know God did hear, and did answer if it was right, in His timing, and in His will. God is sovereign. I also give credit to many others who were also praying in many cases for the same conclusions. A few of our prayers answered are as follows.

Jeremiah 32:17 Ah Lord GOD! behold, thou hast made the heaven and the earth by thy great power and stretched out arm, and there is nothing too hard for the.

Deuteronomy 32:4 He is the Rock, his work is perfect: for all his ways are judgment: a God of truth and without iniquity, just and right is he.

Romans 11:33 O the depth of the riches both of the wisdom and knowledge of God! how unsearchable are his judgments, and his ways past finding out!

THE HOLY SPIRIT GUIDES

Ray and I always prayed for our Pastor and the following Sunday service as well as many other things. On several occasions the Lord would lay on us a particular subject and sometimes actual Bible verses to pray for. Sunday services would prove them correct. I have observed over many years that the Holy Spirit would sometimes lead teachers and preachers to teach and preach supporting topics. The Holy Spirit is real. As Christians we need to open our hearts and minds to His direction. God answers prayer.

> *John 16:13 Howbeit when he, the Spirit of truth, is come, he will guide you into all truth: for he shall not speak of himself; but whatsoever he shall hear, that shall he speak: and he will shew you things to come.*

> *Romans 8:27 And he that searcheth the hearts knoweth what is the mind of the Spirit, because he maketh intercession for the saints according to the will of God.*

> *Romans 15:30 Now I beseech you, brethren, for the Lord Jesus Christ's sake, and for the love of the Spirit, that ye strive together with me in your prayers to God for me.*

> *1 Corinthians 2:13 Which things also we speak, not in the words which man's wisdom teacheth, but which the Holy Ghost teacheth; comparing spiritual things with spiritual.*

BREEDLOVE'S CHRISTMAS GIFT

A young married couple in our church at Forrest Hills Baptist Church, Julie and Lamar Breedlove, who is now Pastor at Central Fellowship Baptist Church in Lake Helen, Florida, asked for prayer for a healthy child after they had several miscarriages. Ray and I prayed that the Lord would give them a healthy pregnancy by Christmas as a wonderful present. Christmas came and there was no evidence that we could see and there was no news. Ray and I did not cease to pray, we just changed our prayer. We prayed Julie <u>was</u> pregnant by Christmas Day whether or not she was aware of it. Nine months later she had a normal healthy baby. I had to ask the husband, my friend, "When did the pregnancy occur?" He replied "On Christmas Day." They now have seven surviving children. (I have seen similar prayers answered for others.) To God be the glory. God answers prayer!

> *John 14:13 And whatsoever ye shall ask in my name, that will I do, that the Father may be glorified in the Son.*
>
> *1 Thessalonians 5:18 In every thing give thanks: for this is the*

will of God in Christ Jesus concerning you.

CURTIS HUTSON - GOAL SETTER

Our Pastor, Curtis Hutson, was a dynamic preacher, a preacher's preacher, and a goal setter. He said shoot for the moon. You may not hit it but if you don't try you will never get off the ground. He reached many goals. He reached his goals by prayer, teaching, preaching, soul winning, and hard work. He set a goal to have the fastest growing church in America. He reached that goal by increasing his attendance to 2,109. He set a goal to have 5,000 in Sunday School. We ran many buses and borrowed others for that occasion. Two thousand, six hundred rode the bus. Five thousand, one hundred and thirty eight were in attendance. He set a goal for people to be saved and baptized <u>every service</u>. (Yes, they were adequately dealt with.) He reached that goal. He set a goal for a larger church building. He reached that goal by building a 2,500 seat auditorium. He was asked how long it would take to fill it. He replied "The first Sunday." He reached that goal. For other accomplishments of Pastor Hutson I refer you to the book titled *"Great Soul-Winning Churches"* by Elmer Towns.

Mark 1:17 And Jesus said unto them, Come ye after me, and I will make you to become fishers of men.

Proverbs 3:5-6 Trust in the LORD with all thine heart; and lean not unto thine own understanding. In all thy ways acknowledge him, and he shall direct thy paths.

Isaiah 41:10 Fear thou not; for I am with thee: be not dismayed; for I am thy God: I will strengthen thee; yea, I will help thee; yea, I will uphold thee with the right hand of my righteousness.

Proverbs 29:18 Where there is no vision, the people perish: but he that keepeth the law, happy is he.

ENCOURAGE OTHERS

One evening as our church was preparing to go on visitation Pastor Hutson asked me to take a visitor from another church with me. Everyone knew about the outreach of our church. This man wanted his church to start a visitation program. We always prayed before leaving for visitation. That night my partner and I were able to lead seven young men to the Lord. One may ask "How many were really saved? All those who put their trust and faith in Jesus Christ. To God be the glory. God answers prayer.

> *Psalm 37:4 Delight thyself also in the LORD; and he shall give thee the desires of thine heart.*

HUTSON/HATCH REVIVAL

Pastor Hutson invited Evangelist Carl Hatch for a one week revival. Church members were encouraged to go visiting after work to invite or bring visitors to the revival service that night. It worked. People came and many received Christ. By the end of the week other churches started to come. Carl Hatch said it was the greatest revival he ever had. They decided to go on for the second week. It got better each day. Carl Hatch stated that he wanted to continue the revival, but Pastor Hutson thought it better to stop. At the last service Pastor Hutson encouraged people to come forward to pledge they would continue to witness to someone <u>every day</u>. Many came forward. I was one of them. I kept this pledge for a few (very few) years.

> *Mark 16:15 And he said unto them, Go ye into all the world, and preach the gospel to every creature.*

KEEPING PLEDGE

My job required me at times to work very late into the wee hours of the morning. I would go home, eat my late supper, pray, and go visiting. (My faithful wife was always available with my meals no matter how late or how early.) I would drive around different bus stops and streets until I found a <u>man</u> I could witness to. I even got out of bed a time or two under conviction to go. The police in the area would sometimes follow my car. One time I saw a man turn down a side street. I followed and began to witness to him from my window. Suddenly a police car with flashing lights pulled up behind me. Two policemen came to my car window. I continued to witness to the man and the policemen while the police wrote me a warning ticket for a tail light which was out. That morning I was able to witness to three people. To God be the glory. God answers prayer!

> *Luke 14:23 And the lord said unto the servant, Go out into the highways and hedges, and compel them to come in, that my house may be filled.*

BROKEN PLEDGE

I learned a great lesson, never, never make a pledge to God that you fail to keep. I broke my pledge to witness to someone <u>every day</u>. I have confessed my sin and I'm sure I have been forgiven, but I'm still convicted when this comes to my mind. Praise God He is an understanding and forgiving God. To God be the glory. God answers prayer!

> *Ecclesiastes 5:4-5 When thou vowest a vow unto God, defer not to pay it; for he hath no pleasure in fools: pay that which thou hast vowed. Better is it that thou shouldest not vow, than that thou shouldest vow and not pay.*
>
> *Matthew 5:37 But let your communication be, Yea, yea; Nay,*

nay: for whatsoever is more than these cometh of evil.

1 John 1:9 If we confess our sins, he is faithful and just to forgive us our sins, and to cleanse us from all unrighteousness.

FORREST HILL BAPTIST CHURCH PARKING LOT

Forrest Hills Baptist Church grew until parking and exiting after church became a problem. We hired a policeman to direct traffic. That helped, but people would come who could not find a parking place. They would drive through the parking lot and leave. We had property behind the church which was about 10 feet lower in elevation. We paved it but the one way in and out was through our higher parking lot. Exiting there added to the traffic jam. We had a small sliver of land connecting the lower lot with an adjacent subdivision. We needed a permit to pave it. We prayed it would be acceptable to all the property owners in the effected area. We then canvassed the homes on all the effected properties. (If I remember correctly we got them to sign a petition.) Nevertheless the county disapproved the permit. On the opposite side of the lot was a flood plain. A road there would not interfere with any homes. It opened to the main road. Ray and I prayed for months that God would somehow provide this exit. The property finally sold to a developer who built an apartment complex by digging flood ponds and elevating the apartments. Ray and I quit praying thinking all hope was gone. This road into their complex was adjacent to our lower parking lot, and a sliver of land which they did not fill. They approached the church with a proposition that they would pave a connection from their road to our lower parking lot if we would not object to their placing a dumpster on <u>their</u> sliver of property. They would allow us to exit our lot by using <u>their</u> road. The church agreed and we had our exit. God answers prayer! (Sometimes a delayed prayer.)

> *Mark 9:24c ...Lord, I believe; help thou mine unbelief.*
>
> *Romans 8:28 And we know that all things work together for good to them that love God, to them who are the called according to his purpose.*

Ephesians 3:20 Now unto him that is able to do exceeding abundantly above all that we ask or think, according to the power that worketh in us.

CHASTENING OF GOD

One time I was able to lead a man to the Lord. He prayed for God to save him. We talked a while longer and he pulled a cigar out of his pocket and lit it up. He looked as if he was intentionally defying God. After about two puffs he became sick.

1 Corinthians 3:16-17 Know ye not that ye are the temple of God, and that the Spirit of God dwelleth in you? If any man defile the temple of God, him shall God destroy; for the temple of God is holy, which temple ye are.

Hebrews 12:5-8 And ye have forgotten the exhortation which speaketh unto you as unto children, My son, despise not thou the chastening of the Lord, nor faint when thou art rebuked of him: For whom the Lord loveth he chasteneth, and scourgeth every son whom he receiveth. If ye endure chastening, God dealeth with you as with sons; for what son is he whom the father chasteneth not? But if ye be without chastisement, whereof all are partakers, then are ye bastards, and not sons.

Hebrews 12:11 Now no chastening for the present seemeth to be joyous, but grievous: nevertheless afterward it yieldeth the peaceable fruit of righteousness unto them which are exercised thereby.

CHRISTIAN SCHOOL

Our pastor, Curtis Hutson, asked the church to pray for property for a Christian school. Ray and I and many others prayed. God provided a closed public school in downtown Avondale Estates, a suburb of Atlanta. It contained a one story school building, a gym, a common athletic field that was too small for any sport, and approximately ten acres of land. Our pastor resigned to become an evangelist. He later became editor of the *Sword of the Lord* which he had previously announced as another goal that he had set. Our new pastor, Bill Pennell, gave us a pep talk and announced that we would open our new school year with an additional new building complete for occupancy. The only problem was that the school year was only three months away. I was shocked to say the least. To accomplish this would take a miracle of God. It would require much prayer, coordination, and approval of our church members as well as a lot of work. We prayed for His help, but as the old preacher said, "The best way to pray for taters is on the end of a hoe handle." We had to plan, hire a contractor, build, and furnish the building in only three months. This required us to design and build at the same time. A couple of us designed a floor plan while we negotiated and hired a contractor. The building would be two stories high with a modern science laboratory, a modern home economics room for cooking and sewing, office space, and more. The contractor took our floor plan and designed the foundation. We checked it and he began construction of the foundation. We would then provide him with details of the first floor requirements. He would design, we would approve, and he would construct, and so on until the building was finished. In the meantime we had help from church members, especially the ladies, in researching and help in such things as to what a modern home economics classroom should contain. Our contract contained a provision that the church could enter a bid for any subcontractor work. We entered zero bids for such things as painting which the men of the church accomplished. God answered this miracle prayer and the building was completed and ready for occupancy the first day of school. God answers prayer!

> *Mark 11:24 Therefore I say unto you, What things soever ye desire, when ye pray, believe that ye receive them, and ye shall have them.*

We later added a bus garage to our school property and used it to repair our busses. The only problem was that the property was too small for our needs and was separated from the church by several miles. We needed to combine the two.

> *Mark 9:23 Jesus said unto him, If thou canst believe, all things are possible to him that believeth.*

MARTA'S ROUTE CHANGED BY PRAYER

Our pastor, Bill Pennell, and our church members saw an advantage to have our school and church to be co-located. Neither property was large enough to accomplish this need. Ray Owens and I began to pray for God to provide this need. It was rumored that an existing private college may become available. We prayed for God to give us this property. It did not come on the market. We prayed okay God give us something better. In the meantime MARTA, Metro Atlanta's Rapid Rail Transportation Association, continued to expand. It was to extend through Avondale Estates. The approved design and location were published in the newspaper. It was to be a few blocks from our school. One Saturday night, at our weekly prayer meeting, Ray said let's pray that God would change MARTA'S location and come through our school property. That way they would pay for the school, we could sell the church, and co-locate both the school and church. I have to admit my lack of faith, but, nevertheless, we joined in prayer to that end. We kept praying and finally MARTA changed their location to come right through the middle of our school property. We serve a great God! God answers prayer!

> *Psalm 37:4 Delight thyself also in the LORD; and he shall give thee the desires of thine heart.*

> *Jeremiah 33:3 Call unto me, and I will answer thee, and shew thee great and mighty things, which thou knowest not.*

MARTA VS. CHURCH

I was given the responsibility to work with MARTA to protect our rights. A couple of us met with MARTA officials and were told we would not receive any compensation because it would not interfere with our school since the rail would be elevated. This unjust, ludicrous comment put my mind in orbit. We told the officials that we would be justly compensated. Ray and I, as well as our pastor and others, continued to pray. The church hired a very reputable lawyer, but we were always ahead of him. We quickly got a copy of the Environmental Impact Statement, and the federal government regulations concerning government grants to MARTA. After a thorough review they revealed that the rail system would have a major impact on our school and that MARTA would have to provide equivalent facilities at a location suitable for our needs. If equivalent facilities could not be found they would have to pay for property and new facilities up to <u>current</u> building codes. This began a process whereby we would compose letters and give them to our lawyer for submitting them to MARTA on our lawyer's letterhead. We thus stayed ahead of MARTA who fought us very hard all the way. Pastor Pennell and I even made a trip to Washington, D.C. to discuss their regulations as both MARTA and the government had a problem reading very clear language in the regulations.

> *Psalm 37:5 Commit thy way unto the LORD; trust also in him; and he shall bring it to pass.*
>
> *Psalm 81:10 I am the LORD thy God, which brought thee out of the land of Egypt: open thy mouth wide, and I will fill it.*

PROPERTY FOUND

Our school property was only ten acres plus existing facilities. We and MARTA began a search for existing land <u>with</u>

facilities. None existed. We began a search for ten acres which could be built upon. We, of course, wanted the money so that it could be combined with the sell of our church, and use it for co-locating all our facilities. MARTA attempted to get us to accept property that was totally unsuitable. We refused. We developed a map showing the location of each of our church members and school students. The centroid was the town of Stone Mountain. Adequate property appeared impossible to find. We hired a consultant to help us find acceptable property. We looked at numerous locations, (over 200) even neighborhoods that could possibly be purchased. Our consultant rented a plane for an aerial search. He found forty- eight acres, an unimproved tract adjacent to Stone Mountain Park, and adjacent to the town of Stone Mountain exactly one mile from the center of town. We had negotiated with MARTA to give upfront funds for new facilities, but they were still resisting. The problem was that they would not give us the money until we began construction. This forty-eight tract was in a trust held by a bank. We would have to borrow money with our church as collateral to make any purchase. This property contained a stream, very rare trees, and wildlife, including deer. It also contained a small hill which Ray and I named "Prayer Mountain." Access was on Memorial Drive adjacent to the West Gate of Stone Mountain Park. The only problem was that it was land locked on the opposite end which could provide a very desirable exit to Stone Mountain Freeway. Ray and I walked around the perimeter of this forty-eight acre tract praying that God would give us this property. We moved our Saturday night prayer meeting to Prayer Mountain. Our pastor and deacons had numerous meetings concerning all our actions from beginning to end. Pastor Pennell kept the church informed. We met to decide how much we could offer for the land. We decided that we could only offer the equivalent of the price of <u>ten acres</u> which we thought we would get from MARTA for our ten acres of land. The offer was made and a higher counter offer was received. Since MARTA was dragging their feet by not paying us until <u>we</u> actually spent money, we would have to get a loan. We decided that a loan payment, if we continued to have problems with MARTA, could put the church in jeopardy so we countered with an offer <u>lower</u> than our <u>first</u> offer. They accepted!! We, with the intervention of God, bought forty-eight acres of prime land in an ideal location for <u>less</u> than the going price for ten acres. We serve an awesome God! God answers prayer!

> *Ephesians 3:20 Now unto him that is able to do exceeding abundantly above all that we ask or think, according to the power that worketh in us,*

BIG DREAMS

While climbing Stone Mountain with my family we observed that we could hear fairly easily a football game down in the flats. We knew Stone Mountain Park often had overflow crowds. What if we had an Amphitheater for preaching, singing, and Christian plays. Would other independent, fundamental Baptist churches support such an effort? We flew a large balloon through our trees and observed the exact location from the top of Stone Mountain in order to point a possible future amphitheater directly at the top of the mountain. We developed a master plan for our property to include a church, school, gym, bus garage, amphitheater, athletic field, relocated sewage lift station and initially buildings for a Christian college. This was submitted to and approved by the county.

Ray and I prayed God would use all the property for His glory. We envisioned a walk through the property to add to the amphitheater. Overflow crowds at Stone Mountain Park could put us in the position of attracting tourists. We could build bird and animal feeders, perhaps accrue some peacocks, and maybe some other animals roaming free. We could have different stops along the way with plaques to identify special trees, flowers, streams, animals, etc. Recordings carried by the people could tell the creation story, fall of man, and betrayal and trial of Jesus Christ. The end of the trail would be at Prayer Mountain where we would have three crosses and a recording of the death, burial, and resurrection of Jesus Christ and, of course, how to be saved. This walk and the amphitheater (Ray and I believed) with a little advertising such as a brochure in the rack at restaurants and motels, etc. could result in many people being saved.

> *1 John 5:14 And this is the confidence that we have in him, that, if we ask any thing according to his will, he heareth us.*

SEWAGE LIFT STATION PROBLEM

Our property had one drawback. A sewage lift station serving the town of Stone Mountain and Stone Mountain Park existed in an area where the church was to be located. It was old and <u>totally</u> under designed for current use and often overflowed into a creek leading to a large recreational lake in Stone Mountain Park. The county had not improved this station for existing needs. At church expense we had a study performed of actual sewage flows and designed a new adequate station to be <u>relocated</u> at the corner of our property by the West Gate of the Park where it would <u>not</u> interfere with our development. We included in our master plan this relocation and all underground utilities including the church. We <u>installed</u> a bypass and point of cutoff for relocating the underground sewage pipes. It terminated in a new manhole adjacent to Memorial Drive. By doing this we had a graded lot, paved parking, and road, and underground utilities ready for a church building. We provided the County with the new lift station design, but they refused to help in any way with relocating their outdated and inadequate existing station. Shared funding would be a future battle <u>before</u> we could build the church building.

> *John 15:7 If ye abide in me, and my words abide in you, ye shall ask what ye will, and it shall be done unto you.*

SATAN'S INTERFERENCE

The County <u>approved</u> our master plan which showed two curb entries to Memorial Drive. The County suddenly withdrew our approved curb cuts stating that the town of Stone Mountain objected due to more traffic being added to Memorial Drive. Even though we performed a very detailed study of our property we overlooked one small detail. The city limits of the town of Stone Mountain was defined by a circle with a one mile radius. The arch of the circle penetrated into our property a few feet on one corner. (We had already begun construction.) This required us to go to the city government for relief. (If I remember correctly it was city commissioners.) They only met once a month. Keep in mind that all our church continued in prayer for God to solve all of our many problems mainly those with MARTA, the county, and the city of Stone

Mountain. We met with the city officials and presented our case. We did not get an answer and were told to come back next month. We did and this time we brought with us a busload of our members for support. It didn't help. One official told us she objected because we would be running bulldozers up and down Memorial Drive all the time. (How can you have a reasonable discussion with persons who have absolutely no knowledge of what they are talking about?) It was clear we would <u>never</u> get their approval. At the same time this was going on a developer had laid out one acre tracts for constructing homes on the opposite side of our property which would open to easy access to Stone Mountain Freeway. Our immediate solution was to buy four acres from the developer. This gave us fifty-two acres. We deeded our small sliver of land in the town of Stone Mountain to a church member and continued with our preapproved curb cut on Memorial Drive. God was in control. We now had two desired exits. No one can fight against the will of God! God answers prayer!

Psalm 91:15 He shall call upon me, and I will answer him: I will be with him in trouble; I will deliver him, and honour him.

James 4:7 Submit yourselves therefore to God. Resist the devil, and he will flee from you.

PROPERTY DEVELOPMENT

God provided us with fifty-two (48+4) acres of prime property. Development included a new modern school consisting of two classrooms per grade from nursery (for church use) through elementary and one classroom per grade for high school with land designated for expansion. It contained a welcome area, offices, teachers' lounge, library, Home Economics room and a cafeteria. We had a new gym which was also used for church services until we could build our church. It contained a portable baptistry, bleachers, training rooms, office area, concession stand with eating area and locker rooms. <u>All</u> paving for streets and parking lots was completed with light standards and underground utilities. Our athletic fields and bus garage were also completed. I understood we had received the most compensation ever given out by the government for such a purpose. Our lawyer said he could have never gotten us that much compensation. After selling our old church and combining the church and school we were completely debt free with thousands of dollars available (but not enough) toward a new church building. To God be the Glory! God answers prayer!

> *Philippians 4:6-7 Be careful for nothing; but in every thing by prayer and supplication with thanksgiving let your requests be made known unto God. And the peace of God, which passeth all understanding, shall keep your hearts and minds through Christ Jesus.*

PRAYERS ANSWERED

Many prayers were answered with respect to relocating our property. Some of the major ones are as follows:

1. Locating church and school together.
2. Changing the location of MARTA rail line.
3. Finding prime, ideal, and very desirable property.

4. Property located at the centroid of church members homes.
5. Purchasing 48 acres for less than the price of ten acres.
6. Property ideally located adjacent to the West Gate of Stone Mountain Park.
7. An exit close to Stone Mountain Freeway, and an additional four acres of land.
8. Provided exit on Memorial Drive after the County reneged on our approved curb cuts.
9. Plans developed for relocating the county's sewage lift station.
10. Sell of old church property.
11. Largest financial settlement ever at that time for this purpose in U.S. (My understanding.)
12. New, modern school, gym, roads, parking, athletic fields, bus garage, etc.
13. Completely out of debt with thousands of dollars left toward constructing the church building.
14. Ideas to include an amphitheater and a walkthrough nature trail to attract tourists for the purpose of winning them to the Lord.

I believe all the prayers which I have mentioned are in no way a coincidence, but all are answered because of God's infinite mercy, grace, and love for his church. To God be the glory! God answers prayer!

Philippians 4:9 Those things, which ye have both learned, and received, and heard, and seen in me, do: and the God of peace shall be with you.

DREAM WITH THE PREACHER

Pastor Pennell had two banquets called "Dream with the Preacher" where pamphlets were provided which included a picture of the approved master plan. Pastor Pennell thoroughly discussed everything <u>including</u> the relocation of the lift station. Also, at different stages of planning and development presentations with questions and answers, written data, and plans were provided to church members. Pastor Pennell saw the future vision for development of this complex and was 100% for it.

Proverbs 29:18a Where there is no vision, the people perish...

SHATTERED DREAMS

Pastor Bill Pennell later resigned and our new pastor was a great preacher but he apparently did not have a vision for the future development of this property. For example, he contemplated selling the part of our property where the new church was to be built on Memorial Drive and building a small church on the location designated for school expansion. My family left to join Corinth Baptist Church under Pastor Don Richards, a great pastor and man of God. My understanding is that Forrest Hills Baptist Church did build a small church auditorium on the property that was to be used for expanding the school. I further understand they did not consider the approved location because of the sewage lift station, even though they had the master plan approved by the county showing the relocation and design for the new lift station. (What happened?) I further understand that Forrest Hills Baptist Church eventually sold all their property and combined with another church at a different location. I personally look forward to finding out (when I get to heaven) what we missed by failing to follow through with this development.

Proverbs 29:18a Where there is no vision, the people perish...

CORINTH BAPTIST CHURCH

Many prayers were also answered concerning Pastor Richard's church's relocation from Stone Mountain to Loganville including a vast expansion and paying off all debt at an early date. Pastor Don Richards was and is truly a great preacher and pastor. He had a superb staff assisting him which I believe to be the greatest. He is now retired but still preaches in many churches. Tommy Foskey, the past associate at Corinth is another great man of God, who is now the Pastor of Corinth Baptist Church.

SAVED BY <u>GOING</u> SOUL WINNING

Lee Watson's wife, Wanda, was saved during house to house visitation. She committed to attend Forrest Hills Baptist Missions Church on Elam Road in Pine Lake, Georgia. After a few weeks Lee consented to go door knocking with me to present the gospel to those who would listen. Lee later revealed he had been in Baptist churches all his life but was hearing things he had never heard before, particularly the doctrine of

Jesus' death as the substitute for sinners. He said he had a front row seat and could just listen. After a few weeks he expressed to the Missions pastor that he had understanding for the first time and needed to call on God in prayer for his salvation. He did so and was wonderfully saved that night in 1982. He gives credit to God for the saving knowledge he learned on visitation. Lee continued to be my visitation partner until he moved his membership to Corinth Baptist Church. When my family also moved to Corinth Baptist Church this partnership was renewed. God works in mysterious ways. He is sovereign. To God be the glory. God answers prayer.

> *Psalm 31:23 O love the LORD, all ye his saints: for the LORD preserveth the faithful, and plentifully rewardeth the proud doer.*
>
> *Ephesians 2:8-10 For by grace are ye saved through faith; and that not of yourselves: it is the gift of God: Not of works, lest any man should boast. For we are his workmanship, created in Christ Jesus unto good works, which*

God hath before ordained that we should walk in them.

GOD'S MIRACLES

God has been, is, and will always be a miracle working God. He says you have not because you ask not. God is sovereign. He does hear us, He loves us, and as a Christian we are members of his family. He is our Father. He is concerned for His children. There have been innumerable (miracle) answers to prayers since the beginning of time. All things are possible with God. Our biggest problem for not getting answers for our prayers is unbelief and sin. I have personally seen people healed of deathly sickness. For example, Bob Bruce, a deacon at Forrest Hills Baptist Church, asked for prayer for his wife who was diagnosed with cancer. She was anointed with oil and prayed for during a church service. Her next doctor's visit revealed the cancer was gone.

> *James 5:14-15 Is any sick among you? let him call for the elders of the church; and let them pray over him, anointing him with oil in the name of the Lord: And the prayer of faith shall save the sick, and the*

Lord shall raise him up; and if he have committed sins, they shall be forgiven him.

Psalm 66:18 If I regard iniquity in my heart, the Lord will not hear me:

MARVIN SAVED

We serve an awesome God. He sometimes answers our prayers in the least expected manner. One of my very best friends in my home town of Monticello, Florida, was Marvin Barber. We both moved. I joined the Air Force, attended college, worked in Jacksonville, Florida, got married, transferred to Atlanta, Georgia and got saved. Marvin got married and moved to Woodville, Florida. His wife Francis still lives there. Marvin worked in construction. He was my pal, fishing buddy, and frog gigging buddy. It was said when we got together our combined IQ was zero. (Probably less.) We continued to visit, frog gig, and fellowship as time permitted. Marvin was not saved. After my salvation I often prayed for my friend's salvation. My job at that time required me to travel a lot to inspect military and civil works construction projects. On one such inspection tour to Eglin Air Force Base, one project was a dormitory, to my surprise I found my friend Marvin was the superintendent. After work I visited him at his motel, and was able to lead him to the Lord. He trusted in Jesus and got saved. He is now in heaven where I expect to see him again. I'm not sure we'll be able to frog gig there, but we will surely see Jesus. God answers prayer. To God be the glory.

> *John 3:15-16 That whosoever believeth in him should not perish, but have eternal life. For God so loved the world, that he gave his only begotten Son, that whosoever believeth in him should not perish, but have everlasting life.*
>
> *Proverbs 18:24 A man that hath friends must shew himself friendly: and there is a friend that sticketh closer than a brother.*

GOD CALLS OUR PREACHER

After retirement my wife and I moved to Cleveland, Georgia, and joined Zion Hill Baptist Church. Our preacher, Terry Poole, resigned. Pastor Aaron King became our next pastor but later resigned. I served with the Pulpit Committee to get another pastor. After many prayers and several potential candidates Pastor Nathan Nix accepted the call. He has proven to have a great family and is a superb preacher. He also started a prayer meeting every Thursday at 7:00 a.m. May God grant this to continue and increase in number. God answers prayer! To God be the Glory!

> *2 Chronicles 7:14 If my people, which are called by my name, shall humble themselves, and pray, and seek my face, and turn from their wicked ways; then will I hear from heaven, and will forgive their sin, and will heal their land.*
>
> *Matthew 7:7-8 Ask, and it shall be given you; seek, and ye shall find; knock, and it shall be opened unto you: For every one that asketh receiveth; and he that seeketh findeth; and to him that knocketh it shall be opened.*

PRAYER CHAIN FOR JANE

Our daughter Jane had kidney failure. A prayer chain was established to pray for her healing. When she recovered the doctors told her they had only given her 10 to 12% chance of living. That was over five years ago. To God be the glory! God answers prayer!

> *Psalm 66:20 Blessed be God, which hath not turned away my prayer, nor his mercy from me.*

ELSIE CURED

My wife, whom I love very much, had Stage IV breast cancer. I requested a prayer chain from our church family, friends, and other churches. She had chemotherapy and radiation treatments. She has now been cancer free for over three years. To God be the glory. God answers prayer.

> *Mark 9:23 Jesus said unto him, If thou canst believe, all things are possible to him that believeth.*

> *Hebrews 4:16 Let us therefore come boldly unto the throne of grace, that we may obtain mercy, and find grace to help in time of need.*

> *Matthew 18:19 Again I say unto you, That if two of you shall agree on earth as touching any thing that*

they shall ask, it shall be done for them of my Father which is in heaven.

1 Samuel 12:23 Moreover as for me, God forbid that I should sin against the LORD in ceasing to pray for you: but I will teach you the good and the right way.

FORBID THEM NOT

I remember at Zion Hill Baptist Church several years ago a young child about 10 years old crying hysterically after Sunday School for help to get saved. A knowledgeable Christian lady told me she had dealt with the child, but the child was just too young to be saved. The child still crying pleaded with me to help her get saved. I took her into a Sunday School room and dealt thoroughly with her. She had complete understanding. She prayed and I believe she did get saved. Thereafter every time she saw me I received a big smile and a very big hug. She always seemed very happy. The young can be saved. God answers prayer even for children!

Luke 18:16 But Jesus called them unto him, and said, Suffer little children to come unto me, and forbid them not: for of such is the kingdom of God.

Matthew 19:13-14 Then were there brought unto him little children, that he should put his hands on them, and pray: and the disciples rebuked them. But Jesus said, Suffer little children, and forbid them not, to come unto me: for of such is the kingdom of heaven.

PRAY FOR KATHRYN

Our daughter and family attend First Baptist Church in Skiatook, Oklahoma. Heath Tucker is their pastor. He serves with his wife Randi. Our daughter informed us of their daughter Kathryn's medical condition and has kept us updated of her progress from day one. The Lord has laid Kathryn on my heart since my first notification of her condition. I pray for Kathryn's recovery twice daily and have had our church pray for her on several occasions. My heart's desire is that many others will join all of us from around the world and bombard heaven for Kathryn's total recovery. Our God is a miracle God! Through our daughter I asked Pastor Tucker and his wife if they would provide me a few details concerning Kathryn's sickness and condition which could be included in this book. The following is their reply. It is quoted in its entirety.

"Kathryn was born with Williams Syndrome, and in her case, severe stenosis of the pulmonary arteries and coarctation of the aorta, VSD, and PDA. Her cardiologist in Oklahoma City indicated that she might have as little as two months – two years to live and that we should take her home and love and comfort her as best we could.

Dr. Umobuarie, Kathryn's pediatrician and brother in Christ said "We will not stop praying for Kathryn until the Lord heals her or calls her home." He helped us find the nearest William's Syndrome Specialist, Dr. Collins, who practiced in Little Rock, Arkansas, and happened to be a leading researcher in WS.

Dr. Collins had treated Williams patients from all over the world. After months of cardiac catheterizations, cutting edge medicine, improvements and regression, Dr. Collins gave us the bad news that Kathryn was worse than any patient he has treated, and there was nothing else he could personally do. He did, however, refer us to a surgeon in California.

Dr. Hanley examined Kathryn's case and believed he could fix her, though the procedure would be very difficult. Dr. Hanley would cut and patch Kathryn's pulmonary arteries in the places they were narrowest. He compared the difficulty of the procedure to the "sewing wax paper together."

We flew to California with literally people from all over the world praying for Kathryn. Every doctor who examined her had told us that sooner or later she would die of cardiac arrest. Over the course of a fifteen-and-a-half-hour open heart surgery, Dr. Hanley patched nineteen narrowings in her pulmonary arteries and fixed her heart defects. However, during the surgery, she suffered a stroke between her T-11 and T-12 vertebras that has essentially left her paralyzed from the waist down.

One year later, Dr. Collins about fell out of his chair when he saw the results from her latest catheterization. He said it was as if "God himself put her heart and lungs together, perfectly." We are grateful that the Lord provided a way for her to be healed. Over the last three years we have prayed for

God to fill Kathryn with joy despite her new limitations and He has! She is the happiest five year old you will ever meet! Five months ago Kathryn was injected with umbilical cord stem cells, donated by a healthy mother and baby. Since the stem cells, she has seen improvement in strength, muscle tone, feeding, and speech. God has answered our prayers for healing of her heart and lungs. On top of that, he has been good to answer our prayers of restoring her joy despite the challenges of her paralysis. Our current prayer is that God will bring healing to the damage the stroke has caused and that she will one day testify with her mouth of the goodness of God. Until then, we tell her story for her and even through a difficult set of circumstances, God has received glory and we have experienced great joy."

> *Psalm 36:7 How excellent is thy lovingkindness, O God! therefore the children of men put their trust under the shadow of thy wings.*

MIRACLE FROM BRAZIL

I recently read a letter from Pastor Rom Rebeiro, a missionary to Brazil. How many prayers have been answered to accomplish their great work? They are starting and building churches and Christian camps. They are seeing souls saved and lives changed. Multiply these prayers and works millions of times to include other missionaries, churches, and individuals for the thousands of souls being saved. Pastor Rebeiro reported that Brazil recently elected a conservative President after thirty years of socialism. Can you imagine how many prayers bombarded heaven to receive that blessing? Their President used John 8:32 during his campaign. God answers prayer. To God be the glory!

> *John 8:32 And ye shall know the truth, and the truth shall make you free.*

> *2 Chronicles 7:14 If my people, which are called by my name, shall humble themselves, and pray, and seek my face, and turn from their wicked ways; then will I hear from heaven, and will forgive their sin, and will heal their land.*

FAITH BAPTIST CHURCH

Pastor Jack Hicks pastored at Faith Baptist Church in Cornelia, Georgia, before he resigned due to health problems. Prayer, missions, and witnessing were emphasized.

They visited on Tuesday nights. They sometimes had fifteen visiting. People were saved. Even though their church was small they supported three missionaries at one hundred dollars a month. The church had a need to paint the church, Sunday School rooms, and the fellowship hall, place hot water faucets in both bathrooms, sow sod, purchase a new stove for the fellowship hall, buy a new piano, pave the parking lot, build a walkway between the church and fellowship hall, provide a handicap ramp, and a few other things. Total cost was between $35,000 to $40,000. The church fasted, prayed, and God provided. God even burdened non church members to give. One man gave $5,000 which he intended to use to buy a car, but God impressed him to give it to the church. A couple (non-church members) gave $2,500. Church members gave; even children worked and gave. When Pastor Hicks resigned the church had no debt. All bills were paid and they had a balance of $2,390.07. Pastor Hicks and his wife, Gaye, are now faithful members of Zion Hill Baptist Church. God answers prayer. To God be the glory!

> *Proverbs 3:5-6 Trust in the LORD with all thine heart; and lean not unto thine own understanding. In all thy ways acknowledge him, and he shall direct thy paths.*

SITTING DUCK

Mrs. Gaye Hicks, a precious lady in our church (Zion Hill Baptist), suffered from hardening of the arteries and was destined for a major stroke. She had 90% and 95% blockage on the respective sides of her neck. She was scheduled for urgent surgery on January 10, 2018. Our pastor Nathan Nix called for a twenty-four hour prayer chain to begin at noon on the tenth and through her early recovery period. She had a stroke during surgery which required quick action by the doctors for her recovery. God gave her a full recovery. Dr. Williams, a retired doctor and member of our church, said that the seriousness of her obstructions made her a "sitting duck." God answers prayer. To God be the glory!

Galatians 6:2 Bear ye one another's burdens, and so fulfil the law of Christ.

Matthew 17:20 And Jesus said unto them, because of your unbelief: for verily I say unto you If ye have faith as a grain of mustard seed, ye shall say unto this mountain, Remove hence to yonder place; and it shall remove; and nothing shall be impossible unto you.

VISION RESTORED

Sometimes God answers our prayers in his perfect timing, but not ours. We consider this a <u>delayed</u> answer. For example: Our same dear friend, Mrs. Hicks, has been legally blind for 28 years. She gets along so well with the help of her husband, Jack, (a retired Baptist pastor), that it's hardly noticeable. (Pastor Hicks still preaches to truckers called the Midnight Crusaders, and in many churches. Retired??) Mrs. Hicks wanted so badly to be able to read her Bible but had problems. Many prayers have gone up to God's throne to remedy this problem. Her Optometrist recently informed her about a new product which would allow her to read. The cost of this product was too expensive for their budget. God supplied the money and the product was ordered and delivered. She can now read her Bible. A double answer to prayer. Prayers are sometimes answered in a different way from what we expected. God answers prayer. To God be the glory!

> *Psalm 81:10 I am the LORD thy God, which brought thee out of the land of Egypt: open thy mouth wide, and I will fill it.*

NO CANCER

Pastor Jack Hicks (semi-retired) was diagnosed with possible colon cancer. He has been very weak and sickly for months. Many prayers from numerous people has been put before the throne of God for him. He had to wait several weeks for tests to be performed to determine if he had cancer. Pastor Hicks declared for weeks that God has given him peace of mind that he had <u>no</u> cancer. Tests results on May 20, 2019, revealed <u>no</u> cancer, but they did reveal inflammation of the stomach caused by calcium deposits. He was told that the stomach problem could be what has caused his sickness and that it is treatable. A double blessing. To God be the Glory. God answers prayer.

> *Psalm 34:15 The eyes of the LORD are upon the righteous, and his ears are open unto their cry.*
>
> *Psalm 34:17 The righteous cry, and the LORD heareth, and delivereth them out of all their troubles.*

HOPE RESTORED

My nephew-in-law, Glenn Carter, Fern Hill Baptist Church in Shelby, North Carolina, was diagnosed with multiple cancers in early July 2018. He had squamous cell carcinoma, lymphocytic lymphoma, and chronic lymphocytic leukemia all at the same time. Survival was questionable. They first removed his right tonsil even though his left tonsil had a more severe cancer. There was a large tumor inside his mouth between his cheek and lower gum and removing the left tonsil would be "problematic." Glenn began seven weeks of treatments, including thirty-five radiation and seven chemotherapy treatments. After the treatments he "bottomed out" and spent ten days in the hospital. He lost his taste for foods and could only eat very little. He lost fifty-five pounds and had to be fed by a feeding tube. Glenn's church had a benefit for him while he was in the hospital. He had people and churches all over the world praying for his recovery, thanks in a large part because of an aunt and uncle's involvement with the Gideon ministry, and other friends involved in the Jewish community. His friends kept reassuring him that he was in God's care, but many did not offer much solace for his being cured. Nevertheless, on February 15, 2019, his team of doctors said he no longer had any signs of cancer, and he was cancer free! God really did have Glenn in His care. Glenn said he only needed enough faith to see His outcome. To God be the glory. God answers prayer.

> *Romans 8:26 Likewise the Spirit also helpeth our infirmities: for we know not what we should pray for as we ought: but the Spirit itself maketh intercession for us with groanings which cannot be uttered.*
>
> *Romans 8:28 And we know that all things work together for good to them that love God, to them who*

are the called according to his purpose.

Mark 11:22-24 And Jesus answering saith unto them, Have faith in God. For verily I say unto you, That whosoever shall say unto this mountain, Be thou removed, and be thou cast into the sea; and shall not doubt in his heart, but shall believe that those things which he saith shall come to pass; he shall have whatsoever he saith. Therefore I say unto you, What things soever ye desire, when ye pray, believe that ye receive them, and ye shall have them.

Psalm 34:19 Many are the afflictions of the righteous: but the LORD delivereth him out of them all.

Psalm 46:1. God is our refuge and strength, a very present help in trouble.

DELAYED PRAYER

Our good friends, Doc and Pat Williams, retired and moved to Cleveland, Georgia, in

1998. They purchased 36 acres of prime property and built a beautiful home and workshop. They became active members of Zion Hill Baptist Church. As the years passed the required maintenance and other concerns have exceeded their ability to continue to live at this location. They put their property up for sale and asked the church and others to pray for results. This burden has continued for the past ten years. It appeared the Lord would not answer these prayers for his sovereign reasons. Sometimes He chooses to answer above what we have even imagined.

Their son, David, is a successful developer and builder in Florida. As he was sitting in his office at Covenant Homes of Florida, two wealthy men walked in "out of the blue" and asked would he consider building homes in North Georgia. Being very much aware of his parents' dilemma and after much prayer, he agreed. His son, Scott, along with his wife and two children, relocated to North Georgia and opened "Covenant Homes of North Georgia." The future of the Williams property will be hinged to this development. God answered those many prayers with a double blessing; family ties in North Georgia and their son and grandson having the ability to solve the Williams property problems. To God be the glory! God answers prayer.

Mark 9:23 Jesus said unto him, If thou canst believe, all things are possible to him that believeth.

1 Corinthians 15:57 But thanks be to God, which giveth us the victory through our Lord Jesus Christ.

MOUNTAIN MOVED

Being consistent in prayer really works. James Smith, a deacon at Temple Baptist Church in Mt. Airy, North Carolina, prayed for ten years to get his prayer answered. There was a mountain behind the church on their property which was needed for additional parking, and a Fellowship Hall and Prophet Chamber. One day a man walked into the church office and asked who to see about moving the mountain. He needed the dirt to fill a hole where a Walmart was to be built. Deacon Smith was immediately called to deal with this man. Walmart was willing to move the mountain and fix the driveway at absolutely no cost to the church. The pastor at that time was Teague Groce – his son-in-law Zane Fishel is the current pastor. Pastor

Groce and Deacon James signed the contracts and work began. Twenty-seven trucks working eight to twelve hours daily, five days a week for seven months moved 400,000 yards of dirt and rock. During this time Walmart was approached by a different person who offered their dirt at no cost and a shorter haul distance. Walmart refused stating that God wanted this mountain moved. That mountain is now under Walmart in Mt. Airy and Temple Baptist Church has its additional parking and a new Fellowship Hall and Prophet Chamber. To God be the Glory. God answers prayer.

> *Matthew 17:20 And Jesus said unto them, Because of your unbelief: for verily I say unto you, If ye have faith as a grain of mustard seed, ye shall say unto this mountain, Remove hence to yonder place; and it shall remove; and nothing shall be impossible unto you.*

An Answer to Prayer by an Amazing God.

H. D. Williams, a retired medical doctor was scheduled for surgery to remove a cancer from his left arm. His church, family, and friends continued in prayer for complete removal. The afternoon before his surgery he was sitting in his recliner watching an old movie, "Little House on the Prairie," in their family room when he suddenly developed chest pain associated with a little nausea. Being a medical doctor, he immediately checked his pulse and discovered it was VERY irregular. His wife, Patricia, was sitting near-by and he did not want to worry her. So, he got up and slowly walked into his office a few feet away. He asked God to protect her and said to God that if He was ready to take him home, he was ready. An overwhelming peace came over him. He walked back into the family room and asked Patricia to take him to Quick Care, which was just a few miles away. Upon arrival, an EKG was quickly taken which demonstrated Atrial Fibrillation with a heart rate over 145 beats/min as well as moderate changes in the ST-T wave segment which indicates probable damage to the heart; that is, a heart attack. The irregular heart and chest pain had lasted about 45 minutes when the EKG was taken. The doctors and nurses in Quick Care would not allow Doc to be taken by car to a regional hospital, but rather called for "ambulance transport." On arrival at the regional hospital, many additional tests were performed which demonstrated that <u>no damage</u> had occurred to the heart. All blood tests were normal. So, what happened? Here it is. When the Pastor of his local church, Nathan Nix learned about the trip to Quick care and the Atrial Fib and EKG changes from Patricia, Pastor Nix called Deacon Leo LaVinka and his wife, Elsie, who called many saints in the church to start praying for his heart as well as his cancer. The very next day after the heart problem, Doc was scheduled for surgery on the upper left arm for a melanoma which was shave biopsied, but the edges were not clear. After local nerve block with Xylocaine without epinephrine because of the heart incident, a wide excision was performed. Pathological studies show <u>no evidence of spread</u> of the cancer. God is a miracle working God, Who is merciful and full of grace! God answers prayer.

> *Isaiah 65:24 And it shall come to pass, that before they call, I will answer; and while they are yet speaking, I will hear.*

> *Proverbs 15:29 The LORD is far from the wicked: but he heareth the prayer of the righteous.*

John 14:12 Verily, verily, I say unto you, He that believeth on me, the works that I do shall he do also; and greater works than these shall he do; because I go unto my Father.

OUR CREATOR HAS NO LIMITS

It's hard to stop writing examples of how great our Holy God is and how he does hear and answer our prayers. I am sure no one, or for that matter anyone, could ever record or keep up with God's answers to our prayers though they tried for all eternity. We seem to forget that the creator of the universe also created our ears and our eyes for us to hear and see. Yet we sometimes wonder if he hears our prayers, and sees our dilemmas. Of course he does! We just need to believe, trust, and obey. God answers prayer! To God be the glory.

Psalm 94:9 He that planted the ear, shall he not hear? he that formed the eye, shall he not see?

Isaiah 59:1-2 Behold, the LORD'S hand is not shortened, that it cannot save; neither his ear heavy, that it cannot hear: But your iniquities have separated between you and your God, and your sins have hid his face from you, that he will not hear.

Matthew 7:11 If ye then, being evil, know how to give good gifts unto your children, how much more shall your Father which is in heaven give good things to them that ask him?

1 Peter 4:7 But the end of all things is at hand: be ye therefore sober, and watch unto prayer.

DOERS OF THE WORD

Saints are those who have accepted Jesus Christ as their Lord and Savior. Saved people whose desire is to serve Christ, to love Him, and keep His commandments. Those who are faithful. To be faithful you must have faith which can only come through the Word of God. Jesus said if you love me you will keep my commandments. The question for all of us is: Do we really love Jesus? Do we? If we do, the Bible says "…..the Lord preserveth the faithful, and plentifully rewardeth the proud doer." Do you want your prayers answered? Be a doer of the Word and not a hearer only.

1 Peter 2:5 Ye also, as lively stones, are built up a spiritual house, an holy priesthood, to offer up spiritual sacrifices, acceptable to God by Jesus Christ.

1 Peter 2:9 But ye are a chosen generation, a royal priesthood, an holy nation, a peculiar people; that ye should shew forth the praises of him who hath called you out of darkness into his marvellous light:

Romans 11:12 Now if the fall of them be the riches of the world, and the diminishing of them the riches of the Gentiles; how much more their fulness?

Romans 11:17 And if some of the branches be broken off, and thou, being a wild olive tree, wert graffed in among them, and with them partakest of the root and fatness of the olive tree;

Romans 11:21 For if God spared not the natural branches, take heed lest he also spare not thee.

Matthew 22:36-40 Master, which is the great commandment in the law? Jesus said unto him, Thou shalt love the Lord thy God with all thy heart, and with all thy soul, and with all thy mind. This is the first and great commandment. And the second is like unto it, Thou shalt love thy neighbour as thyself. On these two commandments hang all the law and the prophets.

John 14:15 If ye love me, keep my commandments.

1 John 2:4 He that saith, I know him, and keepeth not his commandments, is a liar, and the truth is not in him.

James 1:22 But be ye doers of the word, and not hearers only, deceiving your own selves.

FAITH
by
Leo R. LaVinka

It's not feelings or works that saves a soul,
It's faith in Jesus that makes you whole.

Life is like a vapor, a flicker of time,
Eternity is forever. It doesn't cost a dime.

It's free for the taking, Jesus knocks at the door,
If you open, He'll come in, of that you can be sure.

He paid the price it's plain to see,
Put trust in Him and His child you'll be.

Faith in Jesus is not feelings or emotions,
It's coming like a child with commitment and devotion.

Why won't one believe and trust with their heart,
When a world of proof is here from the start.

The evidence is gigantic in history and finds,
It's not hard to know if your heart is inclined.

A look into heaven on a clear night's sky,
Is proof by itself, it's believe or die.

Without faith in Jesus it's impossible to please God,
It's only by His grace that we're not returned to sod.

ANSWERED PRAYERS

Faith comes by hearing and hearing by His Word,
Not to read and study it, can only be absurd.

One reads many books, of that there is no doubt,
Why won't they read the one with the clout?

Satan is alive, he'll deceive your heart,
Don't give him a foothold, you could miss the mark.

Hell is real, it's suffering and pain,
If you don't get saved, you'll end in flame.

Eternity is forever, it's heaven or hell,
The choice is yours and only you can tell.

Heaven you'd choose if you'd only listen,
Jesus is alive, He has truly risen.

We walk by faith with our mind and heart,
To please our Saviour and escape the dark.

All things are possible with Jesus you see,
Put faith in Him, and with Him you'll be.

Now clear your mind and make your choice,
It's Jesus who loves you, He speaks true voice.

SCRIPTURE REFERENCES FOR THE POEM, "FAITH" By LEO LAVINKA

But without faith it is impossible to please Him, For he that cometh to God, must believe that He is, And that He is a rewarder of those that diligently seek Him. (Hebrews 11:6)

For by grace are ye saved through faith, and that not of yourselves: it is the gift of God. Not of works, lest any man should boast. (Ephesians 2:8, 9)

He that believeth on Him is not condemned, but he that believeth not is condemned already, because he hath not believed in the name of the only begotten Son of God. (John 3:18)

For all have sinned, and come short of the glory of God. (Romans 3:23)

For the wages of sin is death, (the second death, the lake of fire) *But the gift of God is eternal life through Jesus Christ our Lord. (Romans 6:23)*

And death and hell were cast into the lake of fire. This is the second death. And whosoever was not found written in the book of life was cast into the lake of fire. (Revelation 20:14, 15)

Who his own self bare our sins in his own body on the tree, that we, being dead to sins, should live unto righteousness: by whose stripes ye were healed. (I Peter 2:24)

That if thou shalt confess with thy mouth the Lord Jesus Christ, and shalt believe in thine heart that God hath raised him from the dead, thou shalt be saved. For with the heart man believeth unto righteousness, and with the mouth confession is made unto salvation. (Romans 10: 9, 10)

For whosoever shall call upon the name of the Lord shall be saved. (Romans 10:13)

Behold, now is the accepted time; behold, now is the day of salvation. (II Corinthians 6:2b)

SCRIPTURE REFERENCES

Deuteronomy 6:6-7
Deuteronomy 32:4
1 Samuel 12:23
2 Chronicles 7:14
Job 19:23-24
Job 19:25-26
Psalm 9:17
Psalm 34:15
Psalm 34:17
Psalm 34:19
Psalm 36:7
Psalm 37:4
Psalm 37:5
Psalm 46:1.
Psalm 66:18
Psalm 66:20
Psalm 78:5-7
Psalm 81:10
Psalm 91:15
Psalm 94:9
Psalm 107:8
Psalm 121:1-2
Proverbs 3:5-6
Proverbs 15:29
Proverbs 18:24
Proverbs 22:6
Proverbs 29:18a
Proverbs 29:18
Ecclesiastes 5:4-5
Isaiah 41:10
Isaiah 55:11
Isaiah 59:1-2

Isaiah 65:24
Jeremiah 32:17
Jeremiah 33:3
Matthew 5:37
Matthew 7:7-8
Matthew 7:7-10
Matthew 7:11
Matthew 17:20
Matthew 18:19
Matthew 19:13-14
Matthew 21:22
Matthew 22:36-40
Matthew 28:18-20
Mark 1:17
Mark 9:23
Mark 9:24c
Mark 10:14
Mark 11:22-24
Mark 11:24
Mark 16:15
Luke 11:9
Luke 11:10
Luke 14:11
Luke 14:23
Luke 18:16
Luke 19:10
John 1:12
John 3:15-16
John 3:16
John 3:18
John 8:32
John 14:12

ANSWERED PRAYERS

John 14:13
John 14:15
John 15:7
John 16:13
John 16:24
John 21:25
Acts 12:23
Romans 1:16
Romans 3:23
Romans 6:23
Romans 8:26
Romans 8:27
Romans 8:28
Romans 10: 9-10
Romans 10:13
Romans 10:17
Romans 11:12
Romans 11:17
Romans 11:21
Romans 11:33
Romans 11:36
Romans 15:30
1 Corinthians 2:13
1 Corinthians 3:16-17
1 Corinthians 15:57
2 Corinthians 5:17
2 Corinthians 6:2b
Galatians 6:2
Ephesians 2:8, 9
Ephesians 2:8-10

Ephesians 2:4
Ephesians 3:20
Ephesians 5:20
Philippians 4:6-7
Philippians 4:9
1 Thessalonians 5:17
1 Thessalonians 5:18
2 Timothy 3:16-17
Hebrews 4:16
Hebrews 7:25
Hebrews 11:6
Hebrews 12:5-8
Hebrews 12:11
James 1:6-7
James 1:22
James 4:3
James 4:7
James 4:17
James 5:14-15
1 Peter 2:5
1 Peter 2:9
I Peter 2:24
1 Peter 4:7
1 John 1:9
1 John 2:4
1John 3:22
1 John 4:8
1 John 5:14
Revelation 20: 14, 15

INDEX

1982, 63
2,500 seat auditorium, 36
5,000, 36, 75
Aaron King, 66
absolutely no results, 25, 26
accomplishments, 36
accountability, 29
advertising, 53
aerial search, 50
Air Force, 65
air travel, 22
airlines, 21
airport, 21
already turned off, 29
America, 2, 36
amphitheater, 52, 53, 59
and go, 19, 39, 65
another occasion, 25
answer, 1, 6, 7, 11, 13, 15, 29, 32, 48, 56, 73, 77, 82, 86, 87
answer prayer, 13
answered, 6, 11, 13, 33, 58, 60, 62, 73, 74, 78, 83
answered prayer, 11, 13
answering, 11, 12, 15, 16, 81
answers, 6, 11, 13, 60, 64, 65, 77, 87
anyone, 20, 21, 29, 87
apartment complex, 23, 24, 25, 26, 42
apartment number, 24
apartments, 42
apply, 13
appreciate, 22
approved, 47, 53, 55, 59-61
area, 23, 39, 41, 54, 57
argument, 31
around the world, 22, 70
arrived, 24
ask, 6, 13, 14, 15, 35, 38, 43, 52, 53, 55, 64, 69, 88
asked, 13, 15, 16, 17, 23, 25, 26, 35-37, 44, 64, 70, 82, 83, 85
ate, 31

athletic field, 44, 52, 57, 59
Atlanta, 17, 21, 22, 31, 44, 65
Atlanta area, 21
Atlanta, Georgia, 17, 21, 31, 65
attempted, 24, 50
attendance, 36
attended, 27, 65
auditorium, 61
August 24, 1969, 18
available, 14, 39, 47, 58
Avondale Estates, 44, 47
aware, 22, 35, 82
bag, 15
balloon, 52
banana sandwich, 31
bank, 50
banquets, 60
baptized, 36
basket, 32
beans, 32
bed, 39
believe, 5, 6, 13, 26, 28, 31, 42, 46, 60, 62, 68, 69, 81, 83, 87, 91, 93, 94
believing, 14, 28

benevolence, 31
best buy, 31
Bible, 2, 11, 13, 15, 19, 33, 77, 88
bid, 46
Bill Pennell, 45, 47, 61
blessings, 6, 11, 15, 16
blood, 15, 16, 86
boarding an airplane, 21
Bob Bruce, 64
Bob Carpenter, 17
bombarded heaven, 74
book, 3, 5, 6, 11, 12-14, 16, 37, 71, 94
Brazil, 73
bread, 13, 14, 29
breast cancer, 68
brochure, 53
broken, 13, 89
building, 25, 36, 44, 49, 54, 58, 59, 61, 74, 82
building codes, 49
bus garage, 46, 52, 57, 59
bus stops, 39
buses, 36
busload, 56
bypass, 54

California, 72
cancer, 64, 68, 78, 79, 85
canvassed, 41
Carl Hatch, 38
cease, 35
Central Fellowship Baptist Church, 35
centroid, 50, 59
certainly, 15
change, 47
changed, 35, 47, 74
checkout, 32
chemotherapy, 68, 79
child, 13, 15, 27, 69, 91
children, 5, 6, 13, 16, 23, 28, 29, 35, 43, 64, 69, 70, 73, 75, 82, 88
chose, 25, 26
Christian plays, 52
Christians, 5, 13, 34
Christmas, 35
church, 3, 22, 23, 24, 27, 30, 31, 35, 37, 41, 44, 46-48, 50, 52, 54, 55, 57-62, 64, 68, 70, 75, 76, 80, 82, 83, 85

church members, 45, 47, 50, 59, 60, 75
church worker, 31
churches, 38, 52, 62, 68, 74, 77, 80
cigar, 43
circle, 55
city limits, 55
city officials, 56
civil works, 65
claim, 15
Cleveland, Georgia, 2, 66, 81
coincidence, 6, 11, 60
collateral, 50
college, 47, 53, 65
co-located, 47
combine, 46
combined, 50, 61, 65
commandments, 5, 15, 88, 90
comment, 48
commitment, 18, 91
companionship, 29
compensated, 48
compensation, 48, 57
complained, 31
completed, 46, 57
completely, 20, 58

concern, 17
concluded, 26
confessed, 40
confused, 24
construction, 45, 50, 55, 65
consultant, 50
contractor, 45
convicted, 11, 19, 24, 40
Corinth Baptist Church, 61-63
Cornelia, Georgia, 75
council, 26
counter offer, 51
county, 41, 53-55, 59, 61
co-worker, 17
creator, 87
credit, 6, 11, 13, 32, 63
curb cut, 55, 59
Curtis Hutson, 19, 30, 36, 44
dark suit, 21
daughter, 27, 67, 70
David, 82
deacon, 64, 83
Deacon Smith, 83
death, 17, 30, 53, 63, 93, 94
debt free, 58

dedication, 18
defying, 43
delayed, 42, 77
descendants, 5, 15
design, 45, 47, 54, 61
developer, 42, 56, 82
devious, 23
discernment, 29
discovered, 6, 24, 85
Doc and Pat Williams, 81
doctrine, 19, 62
doer, 63, 88
dollars, 58, 59, 75
door knocking, 25, 62
dormitory, 66
downtown, 22, 44
Dr. Collins, 71, 72
Dr. Hanley, 72
Dr. Williams, 76
drive, 31, 39, 41
dumpster, 42
dynamic preacher, 36
editor, 44
Eglin Air Force Base, 66
Elam Road, 62
Elmer Towns, 37
Elsie, 86

emphasized, 19, 23, 75
employee, 21
encouraged, 38
Environmental Impact Statement, 48
envisioned, 53
equivalent, 49, 51
escalator, 21
eternity, 87
evening service, 23
every crossing, 24
facilities, 49
Faith, 75, 91, 92
Faith Baptist Church, 75
fastest growing church, 36
Father, 6, 13, 15, 20, 25, 35, 64, 69, 87, 88
Fern Hill Baptist Church, 79
fifth birthday, 27
fifty-two acres, 56
First Baptist Church, 70
fishing buddy, 65
five years old, 27
flashing lights, 39
flood plain, 42
flood ponds, 42
floor plan, 45
follow, 39, 61
fool, 27
forgiven, 40, 65
forgiveness, 18
forgiving, 40
Forrest Hills Baptist Church, 18, 19, 26, 27, 31, 35, 41, 61, 64
forty-eight acres, 51
foundation, 29, 45
four children, 27
Francis, 65
friend, 3, 17, 26, 32, 35, 65, 66, 77
frog gigging, 65
front row seat, 63
future, 52, 55, 60, 61, 82
gave up, 17, 19
Gaye Hicks, 76
Gideon ministry, 80
give, 6, 11-14, 16, 19, 22, 32, 35, 38, 47-50, 75, 88, 92
Glenn Carter, 79
glory, 6, 12, 13, 16, 17, 21, 22, 35, 38, 40, 53, 60, 63, 66, 68, 73, 74, 76, 78, 80, 83, 87, 93

go, 20, 21, 23, 27, 31, 37-39, 55, 62, 87
goal, 36, 44
God, 3, 5, 6, 10-13, 15-28, 32, 33-38, 40, 42-44, 47, 49, 51, 53, 55, 57, 58, 60-70, 72-78, 80-85, 87-91, 93, 94
God answered, 27, 46, 82
God answers prayer, 18, 20, 21, 22, 24-27, 34, 35, 38, 40, 42, 46, 48, 52, 56, 58, 60, 63, 66-69, 74, 76, 78, 79, 80, 83, 84, 86, 87
God was leading, 26
gospel, 20, 27, 39, 62
government, 48, 55, 57
grace, 60, 63, 68, 86, 91, 93
grants, 48
graven, 11-13
great Christian, 32
great church, 27
great grandchildren, 28
great ministry, 18
hard work, 36
healing, 67, 73
healthy, 35, 73
healthy child, 35
hear, 6, 16, 32, 34, 52, 64, 65, 67, 74, 86, 87
heard, 16, 29, 60, 62
heart, 5, 13, 16, 17, 29, 37, 38, 48, 65, 70, 72, 76, 81, 85, 90-92, 94
Heath Tucker, 70
heaven, 3, 11, 16, 20, 25, 33, 61, 66, 67, 69, 70, 74, 88, 91, 92
help, 5, 12, 17, 20, 24, 25, 28, 37, 42, 45, 50, 54, 56, 68, 69, 77, 81
His Holy Word, 27
hoe handle, 45
Holy Spirit, 27, 29, 33
home, 23, 39, 45, 65, 71, 82, 85
humble, 31, 67, 74
ideal location, 52
invite, 38

IQ, 65
Jacksonville, Florida, 17, 65
James Smith, 83
Jane, 27, 67
jeopardy, 51
Jesus, 12, 13, 15, 16, 18, 20, 25, 28, 34, 36-38, 46, 53, 58, 63, 66, 68-70, 77, 81, 83, 84, 88-92, 94
Jesus Christ, 15, 16, 18, 25, 34, 38, 53, 83, 88, 89, 94
Jesus Loves Me, 28
Jewish community, 80
Job, 11-13, 96
John 8 32, 74, 96
John R. Rice, 14
Julie and Lamar Breedlove, 35
Kathryn, 70-73
kidney failure, 67
KJV, 11, 13
knees, 29
Lake Helen, Florida, 35
land, 41, 44, 49, 56, 57, 59, 67, 74, 78

large box of tracts, 21
larger church building, 36
lawyer, 48, 57
lead, 11, 12, 24-26, 31, 33, 38, 43, 66
Lee Watson's, 62
letterhead, 49
letters, 49
life, 15, 17, 18, 62, 66, 93, 94
listen, 62, 92
little book, 21
little children, 28, 70
lived, 19
lives, 13, 15, 65, 74
loan, 51
location, 24, 26, 30, 47, 49, 50, 52, 58, 61, 82
Lord, 14-16, 18, 25, 33-35, 38, 42, 43, 59, 64-66, 70-72, 82, 83, 88, 90, 94
Lord and Savior, 16, 88
lost, 20, 26, 29, 79
love, 16-18, 29, 34, 42, 60, 63, 68, 71, 80, 88, 90
ludicrous, 48
main road, 42

major hub, 22
man, 3, 14, 19, 20, 25, 31, 32, 34, 37, 39, 43, 53, 61-63, 66, 75, 83, 93, 94
manhole, 54
many apartments, 24
map, 21, 31, 50
market, 47
married, 35, 65
MARTA, 9, 47-49, 55, 58
Marvin Barber, 65
master plan, 52, 54, 55, 60, 61
maze, 24
meetings, 51
members, 30, 38, 46, 56, 64, 75, 82
Memorial Drive, 51, 54, 55, 59, 61
mercy, 17, 60, 68
methodical, 31
Methodist, 17
Metro Atlanta, 23, 47
Midnight Crusaders, 77
miles, 31, 46, 85
military, 65
miracle, 45, 64, 70, 86

miscarriages, 35
missionary, 73
money, 50, 78
months, 30, 35, 42, 45, 71, 73, 78, 84
Monticello, Florida, 65
mountain, 52, 77, 81, 83, 84
Mt. Airy, North Carolina, 83
mysterious ways, 63
neighborhood, 23
never go, 19, 58
newspaper, 47
night, 11, 26, 30, 32, 38, 91
normal healthy baby, 35
occupancy, 45
office, 45, 57, 82, 83, 85
officials, 48
oil, 64
Olympics, 22
one mile, 50, 55
one more apartment, 25
one more visit, 26
one way, 41
orbit, 48
outreach, 37

overflow crowds, 52
paid, 15, 75, 91
painting, 46
pamphlets, 60
paralysis, 73
parents, 29, 82
Park, 51, 54
parking, 41, 54, 57, 59, 75, 83
partner, 3, 24, 25, 38, 63
partnership, 20, 63
passing out tracts, 23
pastor, 18, 44, 47, 48, 51, 61-63, 66, 70, 76, 77, 83
Pastor, 13, 18, 23, 26, 30, 33, 35, 36, 37, 38, 49, 51, 60-62, 66, 70, 73, 75, 77, 78, 83, 86
Pastor Don Richards, 61, 62
Pastor Hutson, 23, 36, 37, 38
Pastor Jack Hicks, 75, 78
Pastor John Reynold's dad, 26
Pastor Nathan Nix, 67
Pastor Pennell, 49, 51, 60
Pastor Terry Poole, 13
pave, 41, 75
pay, 32, 40, 47, 49
peace of mind, 18, 78
pediatrician, 71
pep talk, 45
perimeter, 51
permit, 41
petition, 41
Pine Lake, Georgia, 62
Plan of Salvation, 21
plans, 23, 60
pledge, 38, 40
police, 39
police car, 39
policeman, 41
praise, 6, 11-13, 16
pray, 11, 13, 15, 20, 30, 33, 35, 39, 44, 46-48, 64, 67, 69, 70, 74, 80-82
prayed, 18, 20, 22, 24-27, 32, 33, 35, 38, 41, 43, 44, 47, 53, 64, 65, 69, 72, 75, 83

prayer, 3, 11, 13,
  14, 16, 21, 30,
  32, 35, 36, 42,
  45, 47, 51, 55,
  58, 63, 64, 67,
  68, 73, 76, 78,
  82, 83, 85, 86, 88
prayer chain, 30,
  67, 68, 76
prayer meeting, 32,
  51, 67
prayer meetings,
  32
Prayer Mountain,
  51, 53
prayers, 6, 11, 12,
  15, 16, 27, 32,
  34, 35, 58, 60,
  62, 64, 65, 67,
  73, 74, 77, 78,
  82, 87, 89
prayers answered,
  11, 15, 32, 35, 89
praying, 19, 26, 30,
  32, 42, 47, 51,
  71, 72, 80, 86
preach, 33, 39
preached, 23
preacher, 16, 36,
  45, 61, 62, 66
preachers, 33
preaching, 5, 18,
  36, 52
precious, 15, 28, 76

pregnancy, 35
present, 35, 44, 62,
  81
President, 74
prime land, 52
prime property, 57,
  82
printed, 11-13
problem, 28, 32,
  41, 45, 46, 49,
  50, 64, 77, 78, 86
process, 21, 49
properties, 41
property, 41, 44,
  46, 47, 49, 50,
  52-55, 58, 59, 61,
  82, 83
proposition, 42
public, 19, 44
public school, 44
Pulpit Committee,
  67
purchase, 50, 75
puzzles, 21
questions, 19, 60
quit, 42
radiation, 68, 79
radius, 55
railroad track, 24
Randi, 70
rare trees, 50
Ray, 3, 30-33, 35,
  42, 44, 47, 48,
  51, 53

Ray Owens, 3, 30, 31, 47
reach, 21
reached, 36
read, 12, 15, 16, 21, 73, 77, 92
realized, 23, 27
receive glory, 22
received Christ, 38
receiving, 15, 21
recorded, 11, 13
redeemer, 11, 13
regulations, 48
relocation, 54, 60, 61, 62
renewed, 63
repentance, 27
resigned, 44, 61, 66, 75
resurrection, 53
retired preacher, 26
revival, 38
right apartment, 25
right house, 26
road, 42, 54
route, 23, 31
rundown neighborhood, 23
saturated, 23
Saturday night, 30, 47, 51
save, 18, 20, 28, 43, 64, 87

saved, 18, 24, 27, 36, 38, 53, 62, 63, 65, 69, 74, 75, 92-94
scared, 19
scholar, 15
school, 44, 46-49, 52, 57-59, 61
school property, 46, 47, 49
school year, 45
Scott, 82
scripture, 5, 17, 19
search, 5, 49
seed, 27, 28, 77, 84
sell, 47, 50
serpent, 13, 14
serve, 3, 48, 52, 65, 70, 88
services, 57
seven doors, 23
seven tracts, 23
sewage flows, 54
sewage lift station, 52, 54, 59, 61
Shelby, North Carolina, 79
shoot for the moon, 36
shorter way, 31
shortest, 31
shoulder bags, 22
sick, 23, 43, 64
side street, 39

sidewalks, 23
signed, 30, 84
sin, 21, 29, 40, 64, 67, 69, 74, 93
sincere prayer, 17
sing, 28
singing, 28, 52
sinners, 63
Skiatook, Oklahoma, 70
sold, 42, 61
soul winning, 36
sovereign, 32, 63, 64, 82
sowing, 28
sown, 27
special prayer, 26
sprout, 28
stone, 13, 14
Stone Mountain, 50, 52-55, 59, 62
Stone Mountain Freeway, 51, 56, 59
Stone Mountain Park, 50, 52-54, 59
stream, 50
street, 23, 26, 31
street lights, 23
streets, 39, 57
subcontractor, 46
subdivision, 41
substitute, 63
suburbs, 23, 31
Sunday School, 36, 69, 75
Sunday services, 33
superintendent, 66
supper, 39
Sword of the Lord, 44
tail light, 39
taters, 45
teach, 20, 29, 33, 69
Teague Groce, 83
Temple Baptist Church, 83
ten acres, 44, 49, 59
Terry Poole, 66
testimony, 3, 5, 17, 19, 24
that day, 26
that night, 26, 38, 63
thirty apartments, 25
thought, 19, 21, 23, 26, 27, 38, 51
thousands, 11, 58, 59, 74
three months, 45
Thursday, 67
ticket, 39
time, 22, 23, 27, 28, 39, 43, 45,

56, 59, 63-65, 68, 69, 79, 83, 91, 95
time or place, 27
titled, 14, 21, 37
topics, 5, 34
tourists, 53, 59
town, 50, 54, 55, 65
town of Stone Mountain, 50, 54, 55
tract, 19, 21, 22, 50
tract distribution, 19
tracts, 19, 21-23, 56
traffic, 41, 55
traffic jam, 41
training, 28, 57
transferred, 17, 65
Transportation Association, 47
treasurer, 31
trust Christ, 27
trusted Christ, 24, 27
truth, 17, 33, 34, 74, 90
turn them off, 29
twenty-five years, 3, 30
two separate occasions, 24
two stories, 45

unbelief, 42, 64, 77, 84
underground, 54, 57
understanding, 27, 29, 37, 40, 58, 59, 61, 63, 69, 76
unit prices, 31
unjust, 48
unknowingly, 23
utilities, 54, 57
vision, 37, 60, 61, 62
visit, 24, 26, 31, 64, 65
visitation, 37, 62
visiting preachers, 19
visitor, 24, 37
visitors, 22, 38
visits, 31
walked, 51, 82, 83, 85
walking, 23
Walmart, 83
Wanda, 62
warehouse, 16
warning, 39
warrior, 15
wavering, 13, 14
Wednesday, 23
week, 38, 84
weekly prayer meeting, 47

West Gate, 51, 54, 59
What happened? 61
wife, 12, 17, 23, 25, 27, 31, 39, 62, 64-66, 68, 70, 76, 82, 85
wife and I, 18, 27, 66
wildlife, 51
Williams Syndrome 71
window, 39
witness, 38-40
witnessing, 24, 75
Woodville, Florida, 65
words, 11-13, 29, 34, 55
work, 2, 20, 23, 30, 33, 38, 39, 42, 45, 48, 66, 74, 80, 84
worked, 20, 22, 30, 38, 65, 75
works, 5, 6, 19, 29, 63, 74, 83, 87, 91, 93
worst case scenario, 27
wrath, 16
written, 5, 11, 12, 13, 15, 60, 94
wrong place, 26
wrong turn, 23
wrote, 14, 39
years, 30, 33, 39, 68, 69, 71, 72, 74, 77, 82, 83
young child, 28, 69
young men, 38
Zane Fishel, 83
zero bids, 46
Zion Hill Baptist Church, 66, 69, 76, 82

ABOUT THE AUTHOR

LEO & ELSIE LAVINKA

    LEO ROBERT LAVINKA WAS BORN IN 1934. HE WAS RAISED IN MONTICELLO, FLORIDA, BUT NOT IN A CHRISTIAN HOME. AFTER HIGH SCHOOL AND ONE TOUR IN THE AIR FORCE, HE ATTENDED FLORIDA STATE UNIVERSITY BEFORE TRANSFERRING TO THE UNIVERSITY OF FLORIDA WHERE HE GRADUATED WITH A BACHELOR OF CIVIL

ENGINEERING DEGREE. HE WORKED FOR THE U.S. ARMY CORPS OF ENGINEERS IN THE JACKSONVILLE, FLORIDA, DISTRICT BEFORE TRANSFERRING TO THE DIVISION OFFICE IN ATLANTA, GEORGIA IN 1969. HE BEGAN HIS CAREER IN CONSTRUCTION AND HAD OPPORTUNITY TO PARTICIPATE IN MANY DIFFERENT MILITARY AND CIVIL ENGINEERING PROJECTS IN THE SOUTHEAST UNITED STATES, PUERTO RICO, U.S. VIRGIN ISLANDS, PANAMA CANAL ZONE, AND SOMETIMES IN OTHER CENTRAL AND SOUTH AMERICA COUNTRIES.

IN 1973 HE TRANSFERRED FROM CONSTRUCTION TO EMERGENCY MANAGEMENT WHERE HE WAS RESPONSIBLE FOR PLANNING, COORDINATING, TRAINING, AND EXECUTION OF THE CORPS' MISSIONS TO SUPPORT THE MILITARY, AND NATURAL DISASTERS RECOVERY EFFORTS. HIS RESPONSIBILITY EXPANDED TO THE MIDDLE EAST BEFORE AND DURING DESERT SHIELD, DESERT STORM, AND KUWAIT RECOVERY. HE IS THE RECIPIENT OF SEVERAL AWARDS FOR HIS SERVICE AND RETIRED IN 1999 AFTER 39 YEARS OF SERVICE TO THE U.S. GOVERNMENT.

HE WAS SAVED IN 1969 WHILE ATTENDING FORREST HILLS BAPTIST CHURCH IN DECATUR, GEORGIA, UNDER THE MINISTRY OF DR. CURTIS HUTSON AND THE WITNESSING OF A COWORKER. HE WAS ORDAINED AS A DEACON BY PASTOR HUTSON IN 1970. HE ALSO SERVED AS A DEACON AT CORINTH BAPTIST CHURCH, LOGANVILLE, GEORGIA UNDER PASTOR DON RICHARDS; RETURN BAPTIST CHURCH, CLARKSVILLE, GEORGIA UNDER PASTOR WALTER BURRELL; AND IS CURRENTLY A DEACON, TREASURER, AND SECRETARY AT ZION HILL BAPTIST CHURCH, CLEVELAND, GEORGIA UNDER PASTOR NATHAN NIX, (ALL INDEPENDENT, FUNDAMENTAL BAPTIST CHURCHES).

HE HAS TAUGHT SUNDAY SCHOOL FROM ELEMENTARY TO ADULTS IN SEVERAL CHURCHES AND SERVED IN THE BUS MINISTRY AT FORREST HILLS BAPTIST CHURCH. HE HAS ALSO BEEN A JANITOR, YARD KEEPER, AND A TEACHER AT A SATELLITE CHURCH. HE HAS BEEN ACTIVE IN VISITATION PROGRAMS FROM 1970 TO THE PRESENT.